The Rt. Hon. Lord Ashley c

House of Lords
LONDON
SW1A OPW

The last twenty years have seen a big change in public attitudes to disability. Yet the measure of how much more is needed can be judged by regular references, even by Government Ministers, to "the disabled". Many people cannot begin to understand the social model of disability nor recognise that their own attitudes, as well as environmental barriers, create disability.

Despite the progress, an enormous educative job needs to be done. People must be persuaded that their old image of disabled people bears little resemblance to reality. Until they realise that the individuality of disabled people supersedes outmoded concepts any advances will be minimal.

This book seems at first sight to deny individuality, aiming as it does to record and compare common experiences. But with great skill and deep understanding, it recognises diversity yet illuminates common attributes. The result is an enlightening account of personal experience shared with others. And the personal accounts gain a new dimension in the sharing. The experiment, richly rewarding, deserves a wide readership.

Jack Ashley

30 June 1993

There are over six and a half million disabled people in the United Kingdom. 'Lifetimes' examines the experiences of twelve individuals and draws out the parallels between their memories and opinions in the context of the disability community within a society which, through attitudes and behaviour, disables people.

The twelve people in 'Lifetimes' come from a variety of social backgrounds and work in a variety of areas. Nevertheless, they find common ground in pursuing a movement for change in the quality of life for deaf and disabled people.

'Lifetimes' is not simply a story of twelve people but a story of a community - a mutual biography of disabled people.

Included in the twelve is the author Chris Davies, who, in addition to compiling the experiences and anecdotes of others, has also compared and contrasted their perspectives with his own. According to media stereotypes, disabled people are either heroes or victims. Nobody in this book is either tragic or brave. The reason? ... 'Lifetimes' is an accurate reflection of the reality of life for disabled people.Get behind the myths, read about real 'Lifetimes'.

Lifetimes

A Mutual Biography of Disabled People

Compiled by Chris Davies

assisted by Kit Wells

with photographs by

Ruth MacKenzie

and illustrations by

Rigby

UNDERSTANDING DISABILITY

Weydon School
Weydon Lane
Farnham
Surrey GU9 8UG
Telephone: 0252 733167

Registered as a charity No. 297264

Cover design by APG, Farnham, Surrey

Typeset by Riverprint Ltd, Farnham, Surrey

Printed and bound by Biddles Ltd, Guildford, Surrey

ISBN 0 9514955 7 7

Understanding Disability produces disability awareness teaching programmes comprising teaching notes and videos, for primary, secondary, further education and adult audiences. For further information contact Understanding Disability (UDET).

Chapters

ACKNOWLEDGEMENTS

The lottery of fund-raising has meant that a considerable amount of time has elapsed between the generation of an idea of a book for UDET and its actual writing. During this period, the author's life has changed significantly.

When I first suggested 'Lifetimes', my independent living was facilitated by Phil Harris. Since 1983, when I first left my parental home to live in London, Phil was always at my side. I could never have contemplated a project of the magnitude of this book but for the security and stability afforded by Phil. With the solitary exception of my mum no other person has contributed more to the quality of my life. For nine and a half years of your lifetime (and much, much more), Phil, a million thanks.

But all good things come to an end. In October 1993 Phil will be married and living in the Midlands. To prepare for the situation I took the initiative to change the system of facilitation. In practical terms this has meant the transition from one-to-one to six-to-one, as I write. This complex new arrangement only began shortly before it became financially feasible to actually write 'Lifetimes'. However, the combination of writing on this scale and having six new facilitators seemed utterly incompatible. 'Lifetimes' would not have been written had it not been for Kit Wells.

He not only took down all my dictation, but also marshalled all the transcripts of the interviews for this book. I only had to ask, "What did 'X' have to say on this subject?" and he would have an appropriate quote to hand. Whilst it would be true to say that Kit has been a technical facilitator for this book, to describe him in this way would be grossly over-simplistic. Kit is a firm friend and a staunch ally; I owe him much.

Thanks must also go to other people without whom 'Lifetimes' would not have been possible. Throughout good times and bad, Mary-Anne Grant (UDET) has been unswerving in her belief of my ability. Due to her loyalty and tenacity this project has seen fruition. Thanks for your faith and trust, Mary-Anne.

Because of my domestic difficulties, Mary-Anne worked a fund-raising miracle. By securing the financial assistance of Barclays Bank, it was possible to fund and recruit, through Reed Employment, a secretary. He turned out to be Ken Michael Stafford, who diligently transcribed the audio cassettes of the interviews for this book. To Barclays, to Reed, and, particularly, to Ken Michael - many thanks.

Finally, thanks to all my new facilitators who took notes of the interviews.

Those are the people who have enabled my contribution to 'Lifetimes'. But it must not be forgotten that the book is greatly enhanced by the photographic talents of my great friend and ally, Ruth MacKenzie. Without Ruth's photographs, 'Lifetimes' just wouldn't have been the same. I am also grateful to Peter Rigby for his witty contributions.

I have never been secretive about my intense dislike of the disabling, manipulative imagery used in some TV fundraising events, principally the ITV Telethon. Now that it is finally deceased it is somewhat ironic to note that this book has been largely funded by Telethon. It just shows that even the darkest clouds have silver linings!

Chris Davies

Chapter 1

Definitions

This book is about disabled people, their lives, their experiences and their shared understanding of how society disables them.

Well, that's the aim of the book anyway. However, such a concise statement obscures a multitude of other statements which must be clearly understood, if the comments and anecdotes contained in these pages are to be appreciated in their proper context. If these sub-statements are converted into terms of reference, these have to be defined. And that's what this chapter is all about - definitions.

So let's go back to our original statement. It said, first of all, that this book is about disabled people. It may well come as a surprise that what I and the others in this book mean by 'disabled people', is not about physical or mental limitation. Rather, it is connected to social restriction. Perhaps, therefore, further misunderstanding could best be avoided by defining 'disability' and 'disabled people'.

Conventional wisdom perceives 'disability' as a state of physical or mental loss. In very basic terms, social conditioning defines disabled people as those who cannot walk, cannot speak, cannot hear, etc. The difference between disabled people and the rest of the population is usually based upon qualitative judgements concerned with negative comparison between states of physical existence, i.e. those who can walk, talk, see, etc, and those who cannot. The latter are then perceived as naturally unequal and abnormal. Physical perfection reigns - O.K.?

Actually, it's not O.K.. Building inherent negative value judgements on anything to do with disability immediately creates disadvantages. Disabled people are seen as natural objects of sympathy and/or pity. If any of us contravene society's expectations of second-class citizenship merely by seeking the same goals as the rest of the population - such as, holding proper jobs, getting married or parenting children - we are seen as heroes.

Make no mistake about it, the negative sense of difference between disabled people and the rest of the population has had really damaging consequences for many of the disability community. Until recently, many of us went along with social conditioning and considered that the only way to be accepted was to minimise the physicality and to emulate the rest of the population as closely as possible. Integration was achievable by trying to be 'normal'.

This route to acceptability should not and need not be. These days, other sections of our society do not have to deny their difference to be successfully accepted. Undoubtedly, it is still difficult for women and black people to succeed, because our society is still geared toward the dominance of the white male. Yet, more often these days, those few who deny the system do not do so out of obligation to deny their race or gender difference. Now, some people clearly do choose to deny their difference, and white male heterosexual society obviously finds such denial more acceptable. Increasingly, people from these groups are 'out' about their difference and are saying "accept me as I am", and that attitude, and the acceptance of it, happens more frequently than before.

These days, disabled people are also 'out'. More and more of us are saying "accept our physicality as just one aspect of a varied society". In being 'out', we are also re-defining disability. No longer is it internally based as a set of physical or mental restrictions. Instead, disability has an external source in social attitudes, behaviour and environmental barriers. If the world in which disabled people live was not designed on the assumption that it is mainly for those who can walk, talk, etc, disabled people would be free to be equal. Precisely because the world is designed this way, it creates a society in which disabled people do not fit the 'norm'. Therefore, 'disabled people' describes a section of the population who are socially, intrinsically and institutionally discriminated against by mainstream culture and mores.

By the new way of thinking - the social model of disability - we disabled people are accepted as we are; we don't want to deny our difference. Unlike the value judgements inherent to the old definition (the medical model of disability), we have a positive self-identity. Instead of looking inwards and trying to change ourselves in order to be assimilated by mainstream society, we are saying that mainstream society has to examine itself in order to become less disabling.

In all my descriptions of who we are and who we have been, I have deliberately excluded terms which refer to sets of physical conditions. Yet, to some extent, these cannot be entirely omitted. The disability community, as seen by the political self-advocacy movement of disabled people, is a lot wider than is generally understood by the public. Given the social model of disability, our community includes people who are HIV positive, Dyslexic and have Epilepsy. An impairment does not have to be visible for social attitudes to disable people. The political movement of disabled people perceives that this criterion could be used to encompass deaf people also.

However, deaf people wouldn't necessarily agree. To many, disability is still seen negatively. They conceive their own community as being separate from hearing society because of linguistic traditions. Deaf culture is based on the nurturing of a distinct language - British Sign Language, and therefore they perceive themselves as being a linguistic minority within society. Disabled people point out that if sign language was recognised as part of national heritage and taught as part of a curriculum on a par with other languages, deaf culture would no longer be at risk. Precisely because society does not recognise and endorse deaf people's language and needs, means that deaf people are disabled by society as much as the rest of the disability community. While some deaf people do acknowledge this argument, the debate still continues.

The one term which still remains to be defined is 'mutual biography'. Although the focus of this book is on a relatively small group of individuals, whose distinct personalities will, I hope, become evident, 'Lifetimes' is not just about them. They are simply illustrations of a greater truth. Regardless of our individual differences, we have a shared heritage. Yes, of course, our community consists of distinctly different human beings. All of them have experiences which are peculiar to them as individuals. Yet, we also have a common ground, a shared perspective and experience, which is unique to our community. Too rarely has this rich vein of experience been understood by the rest of society. This book aims to begin such an understanding.

So whose 'Lifetimes' are we talking about?

Read on.

Chapter 2

Introductions

How to pick a small group of people who are reasonably representative of a larger community? The easy option would be to be medically orientated and choose one person from each impairment constituency. But that is not the point of the book, quite apart from being politically incorrect.

The people in 'Lifetimes' are here because they are all interesting in their own right as individuals. True, their impairments are different, but that is almost an irrelevance. 'Almost' because impairment does have some consequence in terms of their experiences. But the central criterion is that all of them are people I hope you will find interesting in their own right.

There is a common characteristic. All are able to see their own experiences against a wider background of the disability community. That's not to say all are highly politicised. But it does mean their views are not simply self-centred.

After making a decision on how the selection was to be made, drawing up a list of candidates was comparatively easy. With one exception, I already knew the people in this book. Or at least I thought I knew them, but was amazed at the facts that have come out during the interviews for 'Lifetimes'. I count myself fortunate to know so many interesting people as friends.

The person I didn't know was Roger Brooksby, and he is the first person I would like to introduce to you.

Name: Roger Brooksby

Date of Birth: 3/3/46

Place of Birth: Peckham, London.

Details of Family: Brother and sister, both older.

Parent Occupations: Mother worked at biscuit factory; Father delivered parcels.

Education: Nine schools, then primary, secondary and further education.

Employment History: Serving in Oxfam Shop, working for Rumanian Relief, working at the Bede Cafe.

Interests/Activities: Bowling, horse-riding, swimming, table-tennis, field events.

Next, alphabetically, is Genie Cosmas. Genie I knew of before I met her. For three and a half years, I was involved with a BBC

programme called 'One in Four' and we regularly featured disabled artists on the show. In one of the programmes we highlighted Genie's band, 'Fish out of Water'. Meeting her for the first time, some time ago, we got on instantly.

Name: Genie Cosmas

Date of Birth: 16/7/59

Place of Birth: Sri Lanka.

Details of Family: One brother, one sister, both older.

Parent Occupations: Father, Stock Controller (now deceased); Mother, Housewife.

Education: Four primary schools, then Ealing Grammar, then Warwick University.

Employment History: Librarian, Information Officer, Songwriter, Musician.

Interests/Activities: Gardening, films.

'One in Four' used to be featured on BBC2. During much of its lifetime, it had a Channel Four rival called 'Same Difference', which for two years or more, was co-presented by Libby Cross. If you're familiar with 'Same Difference' you might think you know Libby. Believe me, the television version of Libby is completely colourless compared to the real person and doesn't do her justice at all. This is Libby Cross.

Name: Libby Cross

Date of Birth: 14/10/63

Place of Birth: Greenoch, Scotland.

Details of Family: One younger brother.

Parent Occupations: Father, Headmaster (now deceased); Mother, Housewife.

Education: Three schools, Stirling University and St. Andrews University.

Employment History: Presenter, Researcher, Assistant Producer for television companies.

Interests/Activities: Talking to people, computers, reading, cooking, lounging around.

'One in Four' was on air for some eighteen months before I became involved with the show. But before my professional connection with the programme, I monitored it. My first experience of Ailsa came with an early edition of the programme, which featured her as a reporter. But the television world and acting are only the public face of Ailsa. Once again, learning the facts of Ailsa's life has been a revelation. Basically, this is Ailsa's life.

Name: Ailsa Fairly

Date of Birth: 3/1/62

Place of Birth: Newcastle upon Tyne.

Details of Family: One older brother.

Parent Occupations: Father, Civil Servant (now deceased); Mother, Housewife.

Education: Three primary schools, two secondary schools, Chorleywood School for the Blind, Edinburgh Drama School.

Employment History: Actress, Presenter, Teacher and Trainer.

Interests/Activities: Horse-riding, swimming, going to the gym, tandem-riding, holidays in Scotland, listening to 'The Archers'.

Through my connections with 'One in Four' and through the BBC generally, I became involved with the Corporation's Equal Opportunity activities. At the time they had a disabled person particularly concerned with disability as a part of their corporate Equal Opportunity work. Through the man who used to have this post, I learned of an Equality trainer named Phil Friend, who did some work for the BBC. When Phil and I finally met, it was as if we had known each other since we were children. At this stage, a pun becomes unavoidable, Phil is a Friend indeed! Here is Phil's life.

Name: Phil Friend

Date of Birth: 16/11/45

Place of Birth: Bermondsey.

Details of Family: One younger brother, one younger sister.

Parent Occupations: Father, disabled; Mother, various jobs.

Education: Two schools, then day college, then North London Polytechnic.

Employment History: Civil Servant, Clerk, Welfare Officer, Social Worker, Senior Social Worker, Principal of Assessment Centre, Disability Consultant.

Interests/Activities: Sports, car restoration, motoring, computing.

For the last three or four years, I have been involved with the Arts Council (Arts and Disability Monitoring Committee). Some time after I joined, Paddy Masefield was recruited to the group. Being with him is like being with Santa Claus showing a child around a grotto of goodies. Unlike many disabled people who think much of the time of disability as being commonplace and everyday, Paddy, as a newcomer to disability, just wants to learn. In helping him to do so, one begins to learn afresh. In the course of explanation, re-evaluation often occurs. So apart from the pleasure of his company, being in Paddy's presence is always invigorating and lively. Meet Paddy.

Name: Paddy Masefield

Date of Birth: 17/9/42

Place of Birth: Kampala, Uganda.

Details of Family: One older brother, one younger brother, one younger sister.

Parent Occupations: Father, Lecturer Oxford University; Mother, Broadcaster, Housewife.

Education: Two schools, then Cambridge University.

Employment History: Teacher, Purser, Labourer, Lock Keeper, Athletics Coach, Arts Administrator, Theatre Director, Playwright, Consultant, Committee Member and Chairman on various committees.

Interests/Activities: Water, boats, the sea, marathon running, gardening.

I have regularly subscribed to the magazine called DAIL (Disability Arts in London) since its inception, and so knew of 'Diane Miller'. Then I saw a programme featuring a cabaret artist and actress called Diane Pungartnik. Only just before writing this had I realised the two were one and the same. Diane's contribution brings a much needed cross-cultural perspective, and shows us how disability in a political sense is truly global. This is Diane.

Name: Diane Pungartnik

Date of Birth: 26/3/57

Place of Birth: Southern California.

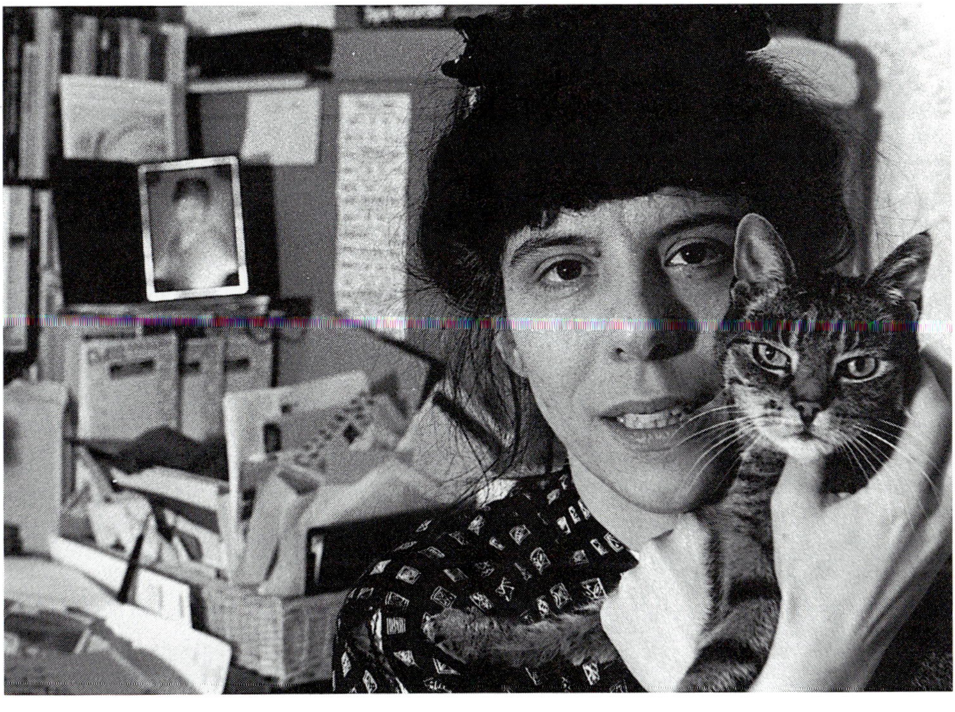

Details of Family: One older brother, one younger brother, one younger sister.

Parent Occupations: Mother, Housewife, Waitress, Clerical Worker, Civil Servant.

Education: Seven schools, then California State University.

Employment History: Singer, Actress, Comedy Performer, Writer, dealing with Enquiries.

Interests/Activities: Reading, music, drawing, writing, history, art, cats, languages, religion, astrology, dancing, talking, embroidery.

Before becoming involved with 'One In Four', I worked for some two and a half years in the publicity department of this country's leading organisation concerned with Cerebral Palsy. After I left, my post was filled by Michael Turner. Because I kept in contact with my ex-colleagues, I eventually met Michael and his wife, Julie. Since his time with the organisation, Michael has moved on to the Greater London Association of Disabled People. During my knowledge of him, his political instincts have become stronger and more defined. This is Julie and Michael.

Name: Julie Turner

Date of Birth: 21/10/63

Place of Birth: Glasgow.

Details of Family: One younger brother, one younger sister.

Parent Occupations: Father, Area Sales Manager; Mother, Housewife, Shopkeeper.

Education: Four schools, then Hereward College, then Hull University.

Employment History: Centre Worker, Assistant Manager in Day Centre.

Interests/Activities: Reading, gardening, baby, eating out, travelling.

Name: Michael Turner

Date of Birth: 26/9/64

Place of Birth: South London

Details of Family: One older brother, one older sister.

Parent Occupations: Father, Electrician; Mother, Housewife.

Education: Special schools, then Hereward College.

Employment History: Publicity Officer, Publications Officer, Head of Information and Promotion.

Interests/Activities: Reading, gardening, baby, eating out, travelling.

My period in the publicity department spawned a long professional association with the publication called Disability Now, run from the same offices. For seven and a half years I have been their television critic monitoring anything and everything to do with disability on the air. One of the earliest shows I reviewed was a programme on Channel Four called 'Hand in Hand'. Its presenters, Sarah Scott and Ray Harrison-Graham, are this country's leading participants in Sign Song - an art form in itself. Sarah and Ray have another distinction, they can lip-read me and are my only independent bridge into the deaf community. Though they are professionally linked, this book is about them as individuals. So first meet Sarah.

Name: Sarah Scott

Date of Birth: 3/10/58

Place of Birth: Godalming, Surrey.

Details of Family: Three sisters.

Parent Occupations: Father, Actor; Mother, Dancer.

Education: St. Hilary's, Godalming, Surrey. Elmhurst Ballet School, Camberley. Guildford School of Acting. National Theatre of the Deaf, Connecticut, USA.

Employment History: Interim Theatre Company, 2 years; 'Children of a Lesser God', West End and on tour, 3 years; Northcott Theatre, Exeter; Unicorn Theatre for Children (actor/workshop leader then Deaf Development Officer). London Disability Arts Forum (Coordinator); Basic Theatre (Administrator/Secretary/ Performer). Presenter for TV Series 'Hand in Hand' and 'D'art'.

Interests/Activities: Reading, sewing.

And now, Ray.

Name: Ray Harrison-Graham

Date of Birth: 29/11/62

Place of Birth: Oxford, England.

Details of Family: Two brothers, two sisters.

Parent Occupations: Father, Pub Landlord; Mother, Chief Social Worker (retired).

Education: Schools in Oxford and USA. London Drama School.

Employment History: Actor, Director, Choreographer. Platypus TiE, PTC Productions, English Touring Company, Pegasus Theatre Company, Northcott Theatre, (Exeter), Unicorn Theatre, Basic Theatre Company. Television presenter 'Hand in Hand' and 'D'art'. Television actor.

Interests/Activities: Travelling, sport, keeping fit, Black issues.

There is one person still left to outline - me. By now I hope it's obvious that I belong to the disability community. Throughout this book, I intend to indicate how other people's experiences connect to my own. So to enable you fully to appreciate who I am, here are the facts about my 'Lifetimes'.

Name: Chris Davies

Date of Birth: 7/8/45

Place of Birth: Merseyside.

Details of Family: No siblings.

Parent Occupations: Father, Quantity Surveyor (now deceased);

Mother, Part-time Teacher.

Education: Three schools (all segregated), Further **Education:** one, segregated; two, University; three, Open University.

Employment History: Part-time Teacher, Writer and Broadcaster, Director of Arts Organisation.

Interests/Activities: Science fiction, popular television, cinema.

So that's the cast. Let's begin our collective stories, beginning where else but with childhood.

Chapter 3

Experiences: Childhood

Being a disabled child is hardly easy. Consider the pros and cons.

Firstly, parents. They come in two types. Rarely are parents of disabled children able to prepare their offspring for independent adulthood. Far too frequently mums and dads start with expectations that are exactly the reverse of those they would have if their children were not disabled. If a baby is born without any impairment right from the moment of birth itself, everything is done to prepare that child for self-sufficiency and independence. Of course, parents of disabled children can be, and are, unprotective. But these are more often the exception.

It's the other way round with disabled children. Parents tend not to expect their children to be able, or even want, to be independent. So, therefore, kids get 'wrapped in cotton wool'. This can become a self-fulfilling prophecy. If you're kept away from other children because of possible cruelties, how can you learn to become a human being? On the other hand, if you're thrown in at the deep end and can't take it, the obvious instinct is to retreat and withdraw into yourself.

Being protective takes many forms. One consequence is segregated education. The thinking is that disabled children will be unfairly treated and inadequately accommodated in an integrated educational setting. I know of many stories of children who, after attempting to integrate, have opted for the seclusion of segregated education.

If being unprotected and segregated are the cons of being a disabled child - what are the pros? Firstly, parents self-select themselves. Those who are likely to be cruel and are likely to be deterred by impairment do not tend to become parents of a disabled child, therefore, parents tend to be what society considers to be the best sort of people - kind, considerate, gentle and so on. Secondly, as all children like to be spoiled, this tends to happen more-so for a disabled child. Whether out of school or in, disabled children can be positively discriminated against in a way which seems unfair to non-disabled siblings and contemporaries. Of course there are a few of us who are experienced enough to manipulate this. Children, say below the age of eleven years, are always less inhibited and therefore both virtues and vices shine through unabated. Thus kids are either more cruel or more kind, more extrovert or more shy and, if you want, more exploitative.

Actually, I'm thinking of myself here. At my second school I was surrounded by children of my age who were intellectually impaired. And what did I do? I didn't use my lack of intellectual impairment to instruct them. Much to my adult shame, I exploited them. Used them like servants and generally lorded myself over them. It was a case of "If you do this for me I'll read you a story". If I could meet myself as a child, I wouldn't like that other me.

All the people I met for this book expressed the general sentiment that their childhood was happy, but hardly any of them did so without qualification.

Chris Davies

One common factor is the strength of parental guidance. It may not be entirely coincidental that most of the people I spoke to are both successful and have had strong parental influence in their life. In my case, being an only child and having a father who, for most of his life, was not physically well, the support came from my Mum. Even though I don't think she had a clear idea as to what would constitute success, she wanted me to make the best of my life. Therefore, when formal education failed, she, as a headteacher, took over. That support, preventing intervention, also occurred in Ailsa Fairly . . .

> "It was my parents who supported me. They gave all the special help."
>
> "It was from all the hassles at school they really showed their protection, from the teachers and the horrendous things that went on at my schooling. At this stage I was actually at a Catholic school, a private school. My class teacher just didn't want to know, she didn't want me in her class, said I was too much trouble. She wasn't a Nun, this particular teacher. But she didn't want to give me the extra consideration I needed. I needed to sit at the front of the class. I needed to get up and look at the blackboard. Consideration, we're talking about. But she refused to have me in the class. So the headmistress, who was a Nun, thought I could be moved-on a year, because I was at the top of the class anyway. She thought I could be placed in a higher level, thus with a different teacher. But my parents categorically refused, because they felt I was going to be under enough pressure anyway without bumping me up a year. So in the end, I remained in this class, and this class teacher was just awful to me; she made my life miserable. I remember going home crying. In the end my parents took me away from that school and sent me to the local primary school."

So, too, Michael Turner.

> "I realise now it was the positive encouragement of my parents and friends that really helped me not to allow people's reaction to my disability to really bother me."

These were positive experiences. But, as you are now aware, support can be less encouraging. Here I'm thinking of the support by the family of Ray Harrison-Graham, who, while acknowledging his hearing impairment, tried not to accept or recognise it for what it was.

"My family was very unaware. They were very supportive, but they were unaware. So there was a great mis-communication."

"I don't really remember if everybody saw my deafness as some sort of tragedy. But I think my family had a view that I wasn't deaf. It was more their attitude. So, even though I was deaf, the whole attitude was as if I wasn't, if you see what I mean."

Ray Harrison-Graham

"But I had a number of operations, six in all. My family were determined to find one to work. I think that back then 'deaf' was a dirty word. It was, like you know, deafness was something that other people had. I had bad hearing, I wasn't deaf. As a consequence, no one even suggested I go to a different school."

With Phil Friend the defence mechanism worked differently, there was no denial he had Polio. It was simply that at an early age he was separated from his family. Firstly in hospital, secondly by segregated education.

"I don't really have any particular impression of my childhood, because I got Polio when I was three and was taken away from home when I was three. So, from the age of three until I was six, I don't have any memories of the family at all."

"The first recollection of my education was when I was sent to a boarding school. I would have been about seven because I stayed in the hospital until I was about six and a half. I came home and did absolutely nothing. Then I went to Doncaster, to school. Most of the students there had learning disabilities. So I was placed with a group of people with whom I had very little in common, although some of them clearly did have physical disabilities."

"It was a very unhappy time and eventually I was actually expelled. I think it was because I was fairly violent. I used to hit people. I have a memory of a kid with ginger hair who called my mother names. I tipped a big bath on top of him, which caused him a great deal of injury. I remember that as being my last time at that school. Interestingly enough, I was on a three-wheel tricycle at the time when this incident took place. I used to have a tricycle to get around with; I'd push the pedals with my hands. I couldn't walk at all."

"So at about the age of eight I came home. I think I may have been violent at the time, because of what we know about today as Maternal Deprivation. I think it was being three at the time

> when I was taken from home and only being visited by my family three or four times a year. Remember people couldn't travel great distances and you only had visiting one hour on a Sunday, once a fortnight. My mother didn't have a car or anything. I think my reaction to then being placed in Doncaster was probably a culmination of all the anger I presumably felt as a young child. I must have been very disturbed, a very disturbed little boy, actually. Being unable to act that out because my body didn't work, I guess I found other ways to relieve my feelings."

No, I didn't react in the way that Phil did. But I can identify with his feelings. My parents were given only one option for my first school. Even though it was local, it was residential and I only saw my parents for one hour per fortnight. I lived for that fortnightly hour. I hated the separation from home. I also disliked the regimentation of being institutionalised; I can remember vividly the anger I felt at being inordinately punished, being unable to hold my bladder until somebody was around to take me to the toilet. This accident could have been avoided by better staffing and more understanding and a more flexible routine. Worse, as punishment, I was barred from my two hours of nightly television. Since, even then, television was my primary source of release from my small world, this was harsh punishment indeed. I and my parents appeared to be the only ones to make waves at this school - others appeared to accept life there as their lot. Thus, in my anger and resentment I was isolated.

Isolation also figured a lot in people's memories of childhood. Even those who were not disabled when young. Paddy Masefield, despite coming from a comfortable, well-off, middle-class background, also felt an isolation similar to the one I've just explained in the context of a special school. The nearest equivalent in the lives of non-disabled children to segregated education is the public life-style of private schools. When Paddy told me of his earliest memories it rang all sorts of bells.

"I have isolated, terribly strong memories of the extraordinary cruelty towards small boys, aged twelve, in a boarding school. Mainly these were intellectual cruelties, not physical maltreatment of each other. I have extraordinarily powerful images of going to my boarding school as a kid of fifteen, getting off a train, wearing an identical suit to every other kid. Then having the two-mile walk from the station to the school. It was almost a tradition that you walked those two miles alone, without speaking to people who were then going to be your classmates for the next five years of your life. I could make no understanding of this, until I observed the seventeen and eighteen year olds in the last year, who were clearly young adults, even in my time, who were walking along toward the

Paddy Masefield

> school - solitary individuals like the rest of us - and most of them were in tears. Going to boarding school, in a way, was like going to prison. It had both the sense of community that prisons, hospitals and institutions had, but with an extraordinary exclusion of other things."

Reasons for being isolated are varied. Libby Cross was not physically impaired as a child but, despite some perks that went with it, she was socially disabled merely by being the headmaster's daughter.

> "I was bullied at school because I was the headmaster's daughter and, therefore, was considered an outsider. So, from primary two or three, there was one ringleader who was absolutely dreadful to me. She made life a complete misery. She would tell on me to the other teachers. She would pinch me and poke me every chance she got, and steal my packed lunch. That sort of thing. I remember this one time in class she took a comb and scraped the teeth of the comb right the way down my arm. I didn't know how to stop her."

Ray Harrison-Graham was isolated too. Why?

> "By the time I was nine or ten I did feel a bit isolated. But the thing was, and you've got to remember we have got a double issue here, we were the only black people in our area, ours and three other families were the only black families in the area. At weekends I wasn't isolated, I had friends because we all stuck together. But in school, when we all went into different classes, I was extremely isolated up until the age of ten."

School life was also a source of isolation for Roger Brooksby. I can only speculate, since he didn't specify, that the educational system found it difficult to accommodate his learning difficulty. Whatever the reason he was constantly on the move.

> "Changing schools a lot had its effect on me as well. I remember once a headmaster came to me and told me I wasn't learning well enough; he told me I had to go to another school. I was sad because I was finally getting to know my schoolmates, starting to have friends. And then they made me move to another school. Then the same thing happened again. I kept having to change schools and I was already having a problem learning. Changing schools didn't help. It wasn't fair for them to keep making me change school; I wasn't learning anything at all at that rate."

> "I liked the school I went to with my brother, then I had to move to another. My brother didn't have to move. I don't think the schools were being fair, making me move from school to school. How was I supposed to learn anything? I think this was wrong. I'm sure if I would have stayed at one school I would have learnt more. Much more."

Well, of course, school life itself is a different experience and one to which we will turn in our next chapter. However, let me finish this look at childhood with a reminiscence which illustrates how honest and subtle children can be towards their disabled peers.

As a child, for most of the time, I wasn't aware of any difference between myself and other children. We played together frequently and happily, except, somewhere along the line, the frequency became less. We played in the morning and then made arrangements to resume after lunch. Lunchtime would go by and I would wait and wait. Suddenly this kind of happening became more permanent. I eventually had to reason out for myself that they were growing tired of restrictions placed on them by being with me but didn't want to say as much. So, the indications I had of being disabled by society was through children's well-meaning false promises and my accumulated disappointment.

Chapter 4

Experiences: Education

There's no better way of beginning a chapter than with a cliche. So let's try this as a yardstick. 'Schooldays are the happiest days of your life'. I first heard that saying when I was actually at school, as a way of mediating my anger against being separated from home nine months a year. I swore then to make a point to remember that schooldays, for me, were definitely not happy. I went to three special schools. Two residential, one day school. All were variously inadequate. The first was institutionalised, the second educationally inadequate. The third, contrary to the trends of many special schools, was educationally highly competitive. But the institutions were wholly unprepared to mix socially and compete in the employment market.

All the schools I went to had some redeeming points, mainly through exceptional friendships made with contemporaries. But, as establishments preparing disabled young people for adulthood, all left much to be desired.

In the previous chapter I described Paddy's memories of arriving at school; mine were of the aimless day that always began each term. The journey from Liverpool to London, where I would change trains for Kent, took somewhere in the region of seven hours. The whole day was extended agony which was only relieved when I met one of my school-friends. Even then, it was only partially relieved because my friends and I would all be in a similar state of being torn between the pleasure of seeing each other again and the agony of being wrenched away from one's family. The despair would only begin to recede, finally, on the journey to Kent where my secondary school was located.

This trauma happened three times a year annually for four of the five years I was at school. At the end of the fourth year my parents had persuaded the headmaster that as I wasn't being given sufficient academic qualifications it was unfair to ask me to leave after four years. For most of that time I was probably seen as what is now known as an under-achiever. School work was a chore. No incentives were provided. At my parents' protest, the headmaster gave me an extra year. I was put in the penultimate form of the school and given the opportunity to strive for 'O' level qualifications. Happily this was a carrot, a purpose for learning! I literally never looked back. This change of perspective totally altered my attitude towards going to school for this final twelve months. Yes, it was still a wrench to leave home, but there was a reason to do so, and in any case I had only another year.

My third school was, as I have said, different from many special schools. It was heavy on academia, but not in my case. It was low on social education. The opposite was true for schools like Phil Friend's.

"...looking back from the age of nine to sixteen, the primary concern of that school was to 'therap' me. It was nothing to do with education, really. I had drama-therapy, art-therapy, you name it, I had it coming out of my ears. No academic work at all. I mean we did do academic work, but it was meaningless - copying, dictation and pathetic handwriting. I think the staff decided these kids were largely unemployable, largely ineducable and therefore thought,'what was the point?' So they would go through the motions of an education. I mean, rug-making as an education? C'mon! I can remember sitting for f'ing hours, making all these f'ing Readi-cut Rugs. I mean, what was going on? And this is at, sort of, fourteen, you know. When most people are getting ready to take 'O' levels, I was making Readi-Cut Rugs!"

"Now Phil, which 'A' level interests you. Axminster Carpet or Afghan Rug?"

Chris Davies

Ailsa's story, though, has a mixture of special and integrated education: while her impairment was comparatively slight - given a few adjustments, she thrived. By the time she got to comprehensive school disabling attitudes to behaviour were beginning to thwart her. The solution was perceived to be a highly competitive school for blind girls. But this, too, had mixed blessings.

> "But when I went to comprehensive school my sight was rapidly deteriorating. Yet I wasn't really scared, just frustrated at times....the structure of the way I got through comprehensive school was, basically, my dad helped me. If I didn't get what I wanted I borrowed a friend's book and my dad would read it

to me. The worksheets he would then write in black felt-tip pen for me, we would spend hours at the weekend writing them out."

Ailsa Fairly

"I slowly got to the stage where I couldn't read my own handwriting, so all my work was going down on cassette tape. It was a ludicrous way to be operating, and still no assistance was offered. The education system offered no assistance and my parents were afraid to ask - because they knew what the reply would be...away to special school! They didn't want this."

"When it got to the stage where we had to start selecting 'O' levels, I wanted to do 'O' levels in Science. But the Science department said there was no way they would let me take Science because they thought I might blow up the school! The

Maths department said I had to do C.S.E. instead of 'O' levels. I was furious with this. There were ludicrous meetings between the school and my parents. The headmaster never spoke to me - even though we played in the same orchestra. I was the one with the huge children's painting book, with the huge letters written on it - he couldn't miss me!"

"I look back and ask, why didn't someone suggest I learn Braille? Or learn to touch-type? But no one recognised or acknowledged that I was blind."

"Chorleywood College was a big cultural shock to me. I had never met blind people before...I suddenly realised, 'Oh, so am I!' It was quite a leap. It was quite a 'ding' moment. They were all girls, they were all so good at Braille. I had to scrape my finger over every little dot. I was amazed."

"I hated going to this school..used to going home for lunch every day...comprehensive had been a mixed school...I was going home about every six weeks...there was a vast difference in levels of maturity...they were so clever. They were streaks ahead of me, I mean academically...there was a real sense of the selected few...I was studying for 'A' levels and the only way I could study for it was through Braille, everything was geared towards Braille. And I was just learning it...it was horrendous."

"...I ended up having to drop subject after subject, because I couldn't cope...I saw myself as a total failure. It was a very unhappy time for me ..in the end I got six 'O' levels and one 'A' level."

"I was a bit of a loner at this school. I just withdrew into myself. They'd all been together since first year, and then I arrived....I just stayed alone and worked and worked...I became anorexic while I was there. My whole perspective on life was skew whiff...I became obsessed with food and with work. It was the only thing I could control in my life. My dad had died. My eyesight had deteriorated. I was at a school I didn't like. I felt I was a failure. So, in the end, I left."

The schools attended by Libby, Genie, Diane and Paddy were fairly orthodox for non-disabled children. The factor that binds them all is the almost complete absence of disabled children in their school life. Almost, but not quite."

"...I can remember one disabled person, when I was about twelve. I can remember being quite jealous. I can remember he had polio. I can remember he walked with an iron brace on his leg...my jealousy was, he was in the first cricket team and I was only in the second." (Paddy)

"...I do remember a disabled boy with polio...I remember he used crutches..he was just someone who was knocking around on crutches." (Diane)

"Maybe I remember, very vaguely, a child who was deaf.. I had very little contact with disability when I was young." (Genie)

For Michael and Julie Turner school was a mixed blessing.

"...I chose to attend Thomas Delarue...not only did I get an education there, I also found my confidence and began to become more independent." (Julie)

"I did have some good friends later at school and, yes, some of them were disabled...looking back, I really quite enjoyed school. I went to a special school with smaller classes and, as a result, got more attention than I would have had in a 'normal' school...the quality of education was not as good as it should have been...the 'more' disabled, in my opinion, didn't receive the attention they needed....being educated in special schools does tend to segregate the disabled from society and this type

Ray Harrison-Graham

of segregation is more disabling than the disability itself...I did miss being integrated with 'normal' people...I really worked hard at my 'A' levels, but I did wonder the point of it all, after a while...what was the point of being a workaholic...I was never really over-ambitious." (Michael)

Ray, like Michael, often didn't see any point in education. Ray, though, reacted differently.

"I was expelled from most of my schools previously, mostly because I was very badly behaved..I suppose if there was any showing of the frustrations of deafness they came across through my behaviour...you had to be 'extra' than everybody else...you can't wear a hearing aid that looks like a small fridge...and you have to do something that makes you look cool...so, for me it was bad behaviour. And skiving, because, basically, I never went to class...looking back I don't regret not staying in school. I guess it's because I've been very lucky, every time I skived at school I didn't just skive to go and play football. I used to go into the local theatre, it was part of a youth theatre. So I'd be either writing plays or directing plays, or planning my next one for the next time I skived off school. So, ironically, I was doing my study for what I ended up doing - drama!"

For Sarah Scott the impetus of rebellion was not needed in order to bring the drama of theatrical experience into her life. Sarah was born into a family where the children had deafness inherent. It's a wonder then that her choice of education was via a ballet school and then drama school. But here, too, disabling attitudes to her impairment have a varying degree of influence.

> "...everyone would turn round and watch me put my hearing aid in.. 'Is Sarah ready?...Sarah's ready? O.K. let's start'. So, of course I immediately didn't like my hearing aid or the fact that I was different in any way. So, at playtime I would rip the hearing aid out and not hear what the hell was going on...I went to a regular school.. it became very evident that I was struggling...I just sat at the back of the class..when I was eight I went to ballet school, it was in ballet school that things changed."

> "The small class I joined meant I had the kind of attention I needed - and this meant my school work began to go very well...going to ballet school had been my choice, I had been dancing since I was four...there was no question of what I had to do, it was demonstrated, so I could see what exercise I had to do. I could see how you position yourself. And I could do it. Also I loved music. So that was where I felt at home. There was nothing to worry about."

> "At drama school....they weren't helping to find ways round my not hearing. For example, I hated improvisation; I couldn't do it because things like improvisation meant you don't know what somebody is going to say. Nobody is speaking directly to you. So there was no awareness at all for me. So I couldn't do it...at that time I was always very apologetic about it when I said 'Look, I can't hear'".

School life for me has no relevance to 'normal adolescence'. When you're tucked away among sixty or so people with Cerebral Palsy for nine months of every twelve outside a small town in the Kent countryside, how could that possibly relate to young adulthood? Well, within it's confines I suppose, unlike other school contemporaries, we did have a form of stunted adolescence. But that's another story....

Chapter 5

Experiences: Adolescence

The phase of becoming an adult is often characterised by either rebellion or blossoming of personality. Both feature amongst the people I spoke to. Ironically, neither was presumably present in my adolescence.

One of the rebels was Libby Cross. Although, as a youngster, she had been a bit of a tomboy, she nevertheless felt the restrictions of being a headmaster's daughter. As a teenager though, these restrictions were shed.

> "..I enjoyed having a few more friends, because I no longer felt I was being bullied...my memories of secondary school were ones of school dances and of not being quite so shy and becoming more of a rebel... the only reason I wasn't given the belt like everyone else was because I was the headmaster's daughter. And suddenly I remember I thought I had one up on every one else...I did have my first boyfriend when I was in secondary school. I remember there were problems with that

relationship because I was Protestant and he was Catholic. In this small town in which we lived, this was not the done thing. But we went out with each other for about a year and a half."

Libby Cross

As teenagers, both Libby and Genie were still non-disabled. In Genie's case this enabled her to be a more conventional teenage rebel.

"As I became older an interest in boys developed, my school just didn't feature...I hanged (sic) out with friends and we went to discos and things...I remember I started smoking at the age of thirteen, also I remember drinking alcohol at that time. So all the negative influences of society were hitting me at a very

> young age...I wasn't very close to my mother, so maybe I didn't listen to what she was saying...I was a bit of a rebel as I grew older as well..."

> "I failed my 'A' levels the first time round, but this was due to having a hard time from the kids I hanged (sic) out with ....I remember I almost had a nervous breakdown because I decided I didn't want to hang out with certain girls at school any more. I wasn't going to discos and things. I realised it was a waste of time. And they didn't take too kindly to that, they became quite cruel to me and unkind...it affected me quite badly...when I got to University I hanged (sic) out a lot in the drinking scenes, smoking dope and drug scenes, so I was a rebel and didn't take myself that seriously. And I think I had a lot of mess from my childhood I had to deal with and get out of my system, and that's what made me rebel so much and go in such an extreme way. But, apart from that, I did pass my degree."

Also amongst the adolescent rebels was Phil Friend. In fact his rebellion started much earlier.

> "When I came home I just dossed. I don't remember this but my mother tells me it was her decision to remove me from school because I was clearly very unhappy there. I'm not sure that's true. I actually believe she was told I couldn't come back. But she sees it as something different."

Ray Harrison-Graham was also going against the grain, as we have seen before.

> "So, by the time I was a teenager, I wasn't confused. I was so set on my career. I was so acting crazy; I had a real goal in life. As far as the deafness was concerned, it was just an irritating thing because it was slowly getting worse - it meant I kept missing conversations. But I was such a loud-mouth by then, I didn't notice....I auditioned for drama school and didn't tell them I

was deaf..I got away with it for a time then my hearing went altogether...the school told me to go away and get my hearing and teeth sorted out. So I went away and I didn't sort out either. Their attitude made me really angry."

Adolescence is also characterised by a growing sense of difference. Teenagers may be more subtle than children because inhibitions are setting in. But being a teenager means you're more sensitive.

For Ray and Michael Turner a sense of difference was heightened.

"The realisation (that I was deaf) would be stronger when I met new people. As a result I developed one-to-one conversations. But it wasn't until later I realised why." (Ray)

"...being at University was a great challenge, it felt good to be around able-bodied people. Funny how they complain all the time. They always seem dissatisfied with themselves. They aren't disabled. They are the people with all the freedom and they always seem dissatisfied with themselves. I often wonder what their problem really is." (Michael)

This sense of difference, for some, has a positive effect. Adolescence proved to be a time when new horizons were perceived. It was certainly the case for Julie Turner.

"I attended Hereward College for disabled people for about two years...this was really good for me. It really opened my eyes to discrimination. Looking back, it was really during this time I did a lot of things able-bodied people take for granted, like going to the pub for a drink with friends. It was during this time I learnt to drive - a great asset to me."

For Paddy Masefield new horizons were perceived, although he was not disabled at this stage.

"I got very hooked on the theatre from about the age of thirteen. What really surprised me was that it had practically all the things I had been totally denied in my life. There were actually people of the opposite gender. Because it was in the midst of working backstage there were actually people walking around without many clothes on; speaking a different language, swearing, drinking and all the things I just wasn't allowed to have any knowledge of. It was like a totally magical world."

"So the moment I left school I was filled with an incredible sense of curiosity, which still exists to this day; there were just a thousand and one things I wanted to do. And then the most bizarre thing happened. Four weeks after leaving school, I found myself teaching five to eleven year olds in a private school, without any qualifications or experience as a teacher."

Teenage life is often angst-filled. Even if nothing spectacular happens it is an awkward time growing up. However, for three of the people I spoke to it was particularly awkward. For Libby, Diane and Ailsa it was the time for the trauma of losing a parent. And it had to be faced. In Ailsa's case because her father had been especially instrumental in enabling her to feel as unaffected by society as possible.

"And then my dad died. I, basically, came home from school one day and he was gone. This turned the whole of my life upside down. It's a real watershed in my life, for lots of reasons. I mean I was very close to my dad; I was a real sort of daddy's girl. But also for practical things, he was the one who had really supported me at school. He was practical and he had the skills. My mum was unable to assist with my school work because she had a lousy education herself."

Libby, too, talks about being a daddy's girl, but in the manner of her father's illness there was an irony.

> "My father got ill with cancer and was in the hospital for a long time, in and out over a period of two or three years. At the time I didn't realise how difficult it was, but it was really difficult. I also hadn't realised how much of a daddy's girl I was until he was away at the hospital and I didn't have him around every day.....the real irony of his illness was that he had Lymphoma, which affects the spinal cord. And it was once said when he was recuperating from an operation, that he would be a wheelchair user when he came home. I remember thinking clearly I didn't want a father who was a wheelchair user. I had terrible guilt over that after my accident."

I emerged from my school in Kent five years older than I had been when I first entered that cloistered circle. But, apart from the onset of puberty, and the attainment of my academic qualifications, I was probably a thirteen year old in an eighteen year old's body. Yes, it's true that I had risked the wrath of the upholders of convention in the school by attempting clandestine relationships with fellow students but that's as far as the rebellion went. Let's be absolutely clear, my angst as a rebel amounted to a few snatched moments of holding hands and stealing kisses when staff had their backs turned. Big deal!

As far as you or I are concerned, although I now had a sense of incentive for academic pursuits, I had little or no clear intention as to how this could be put into action. I certainly had absolutely no notion as to what purpose I could use any qualifications in terms of meaningful employment. What a way to start adulthood!

Chapter 6

Experiences: Adulthood

At what age is one an adult? It used to be twenty-one, now it's eighteen years. I would say that for Libby Cross adulthood began at seventeen. A motor-bike accident was to change her life. The supreme irony is that it occurred in 1981 - International Year of the Disabled.

Now, Libby takes it for granted. So much so that in the section of the questionnaire marked 'significant dates' she almost omitted this landmark. It was a shattering experience, made all the more so because she had to adapt to her new identity without any help. Here's how she remembers the events that made her a different person.

> "I had intended to go on...to Glasgow Tech. to do Social Science. Then I had my accident, which put a halt to my going. I was seventeen. Of course, this was a major turning point in my life. But seventeen to eighteen is generally a major turning point in everyone's life. The accident just kind of focussed the turning point a bit more sharply. I'm sure if I hadn't had the accident I

Libby Cross

would have gone straight on to college. And I would have done a really boring degree - ended up being a social worker, married with three children and still living in the same community in which I grew up. When I compare that to what I did do, even having the accident, I think it was a good thing to have had the accident. But, on the other hand, at seventeen, I had the accident and thought, Oh, my God. I'm seventeen and I am confined to a wheelchair for the rest of my life. What on earth am I going to do?"

"I was also dealing with losing friends, dealing with not having any rehabilitation, dealing with having no encouragement. There was no major help at all. At the time, I didn't get my head round having the accident at all. For at least two years I was a complete disaster area. I spent four months in hospital, where they were very supportive - because nurses are like that.... Now the ironic part...having had my accident in 1981, which was named the International Year of the Disabled Person, I remember I heard an appeal on the television and had sent off a cheque. Then there I was, later to have my own disabling accident - a couple of months later it's me!."

Libby was not the only one to obtain an impairment during early adulthood. Hear Genie Cosmas's account of how M.S. entered her life.

"...I got M.S. and felt very peculiar. I didn't really understand what was going on...I was about twenty-four when this started to happen...I got these pains at the back of my head that I've had ever since. The left side of my body felt numb. I actually got much worse. Eventually I got double-vision and couldn't walk properly. I went back to my folks and got admitted to hospital. They pumped me full of steroids and, for a time, I actually got better. So there was this cycle of having attacks and getting steroids and this went on for the next six years."

"I still didn't know that I had M.S. I thought I was going out of my mind....they wanted to send me to a psychiatric hospital and have me go through some sort of psychiatric analysis because they said it was all in the head. Of course it was all in the head actually, because M.S. does affect the brain, but they did not understand or know what was going on....I got very ill. It was then, when I went into hospital, that I was diagnosed as having M.S.... because I hadn't known what was going on I felt very isolated and turned to music as a way of releasing all the frustrations and difficulties I had dealing with what was going on in my head."

For Libby, the solution to her trauma was found in her University colleagues.

> "...my self-image was terrible. I didn't know how to hold a conversation...I did not feel I had anything of value to offer anyone. I felt completely unattractive, asexual, colourless.... But I had some very good friends at University. They refused to allow me to carry on in my solitude. They refused to allow me to get away with hiding behind this front. They got to know me, in spite of all my best efforts not to let them, because I felt of such low value. But I made good friends. I started to do better at the work. I started to find satisfaction in getting good marks. This got my mind going. My emotional life I decided to put on the back-burner in favour of my intellectual life. It really took off."

However, higher education had just been completed when Epilepsy entered into Diane Pungartnik's life.

Diane Pungartnik

> "When my Epilepsy began it was a strange thing that happened out of the blue. Because it had only been one seizure, and anyone can have a seizure, they decided they wouldn't bother investigating my brain waves, or putting me on drugs - they just let me go. Then I was eighteen and had the summer off before I went to University... I don't think the word Epilepsy was mentioned...I just knew that I had to be careful, not to get overworked, to get enough sleep and not to cause that to happen again. And it was very strange. I went through four years of University with absolutely nothing happening. I was under enormous strain at the time ...this went on day after day...then the summer after I got my degree, for no reason whatsoever: bonk! I had one. No warning, I just blacked out."

One way, or another, for our group, adulthood was a revelation. For Phil Friend, like myself, it was a time of revelation. In the event we were ill-prepared for a competitive world.

> "I left school feeling good about myself, I left as head boy. I was troop leader in the scouts, I was team master of everything moving and I thought that was brilliant...I left school at sixteen. I went into the Civil Service ...I didn't know what the Daily Telegraph was, I didn't know what a telephone was, I didn't know where to get new ferrules for my crutches, or new tyres for my wheelchair...I went from being head boy, team captain and all that to feeling totally insecure. And it frightened the shit out of me."

For both Julie and Michael Turner, too, it was a time when they came to understand more fully the complexities of life in a disabling society.

"Like any person, becoming an adult means you are free to make choices and decisions you were not able to make before, and this is good. I think in some ways it is harder for society to accept disabled adults doing the 'normal' things in life. This can be very difficult to take at times." (Julie)

"..I discovered as I got older and finished school there were less opportunities for me than I thought I would have. Looking back, it's amazing how very unconscious I was of my disability with regard to the opportunity that would be available to me, that my disability would be used as an excuse with regard to employment....after having succeeded at University, I felt fairly confident I could succeed at most things." (Michael)

Our society has many stereotypes about disability. One that sticks to people with learning difficulty is that they are not sensitive to how others react to them. Once again, let Roger Brooksby belie that myth.

"As I've grown older people still react to my disability. Some people will help me if I need it. But the average person still doesn't want to know. I guess it just depends on the way a person is brought up, I suppose. There are some peculiar people in the world."

For Ailsa Fairly and Sarah Scott, early adulthood meant the beginning of their professional careers. Of course, choosing a profession and managing to pursue it do not necessarily follow if you're a disabled person. How did Sarah and Ailsa buck the trend?

"I knew that's where I belonged (the British Theatre of the Deaf), that it would answer all the questions I had about work. I knew I would be somewhere I belonged. I wouldn't have all these people telling me I couldn't do it...sign language gave me a sense of belonging. The moment I saw it I belonged there...I

Sarah Scott

should have, without question, been given sign language earlier...the moment I saw it I swallowed it up..I had no worries about being deaf because sign language gave me strength." (Sarah)

"I actually conned my way into Drama School. They thought I could actually see something. I arrived early, because I knew it was going to be a group thing and then an interview. I met this rather chatty young woman and when they came up to us I just pretended to look in my bag. I whispered to her 'Can I take your arm?' So I organised her as the help I needed. In retrospect, they must have spent the first half hour or so wondering which one was blind. I was still aware of shapes so I

> could manoeuvre around. In the end they took me on because I convinced them I could still play sighted parts. And they wanted publicity out of it for their course, which they got. I wanted a Drama school training - which I got!" (Ailsa)

Early childhood for me can be summed up in the word 'study'. I became a perpetual mature student. I enjoyed learning and knew that the qualifications were worth gaining. But I didn't have a clue as to what use I would put them. Nobody gave me any indication as to what kind of work I would do. So I went through half a conventional University career, which had to be abandoned because of my over-zealous need to compete on an equal basis, and a five year Open University degree. The end of this academic period concluded in 1981. Yes, that year again! During that twelve months there were many television programmes about disability, but only one that was actually made by disabled people. That programme changed my life and gave me a career.

Chapter 7

Experiences: Employment

Finding a satisfactory job, even at the best of financial times, is hardly easy for anyone. For disabled people prejudices, myths, stereotypes and preconceptions all contribute to make us bottom of the list when it comes to desirable candidates for potential employment. Disabled people had always had a higher rate of unemployment than the rest of the population.

Even though. There's a quota system which is supposed to ensure a certain percentage of disabled people are employed. Maintaining the quotas is a legal requirement. Yet no government has diligently policed it and it is far too easy to escape the responsibilities which are involved. Until it is legally impossible to discriminate on the grounds of disability, the same people are going to find other ways to enable a disabling society that would prefer not to employ us.

So how did our 'Lifetimes' group fare? Most of them are artists, where commercial constraints are not particularly prevalent; nevertheless, discrimination has to be overcome. You read in the previous chapter how Ailsa conned her way into Drama school - how did she then go about gaining work in the profession she chose?

> "I knew it was going to be difficult, but it was difficult for everybody. I mean there are too many actors. But I was going to do it....I went to auditions and met directors and so on...what eventually happened was that, at a final performance day (at Drama school), one of the artistic directors of a Rep company was aware of me and set up the initial thought of me working with disabled people. He had seen an advertisement in 'The Stage' for Graeae, which was advertising for disabled actors. I followed it up and went to work for Graeae. It turned out to be a very challenging experience. It challenged all the things I had learned in Drama school. We had countless debates on standards - whether disabled people should play disabled parts, all those ideas....slowly I was becoming aware of myself and more aware of the political aspects of disability."

For Genie, the constraints of M.S. were also influencing her choice of work.

> "I didn't have any great ambitions at that time...I didn't work in terms of having a real job; I just worked at studying my music. I went to these sort of community schools around London, improving my sax. The songs I wrote were mainly about having M.S....I met Zandra, we started working together and doing gigs, most of them mainstream actually. Then I saw this ad in 'DAIL' with work contacts. So I contacted them and we got together to do a gig. More work followed from there...most of my work is through Disability Art. I am happy with this."

Genie Cosmas

Being unprepared as he was for work, Phil Friend went through a succession of jobs until he found where he was most comfortable.

> "Originally I went into the Civil Service ...they sent me to Brookgreen Day College...it helped me catch up on the education I missed...I applied for a job in Hammersmith London Borough Council... I got the job, but it turned out to be more pen-pushing, filling in bloody forms...I got a job as a Welfare Officer..it was like putting on a glove that fitted...I had two hundred old people who were my responsibility...it was basically social work, it was the most rewarding time for me. I remember feeling very pleased I was given the opportunity to do it...I enjoyed the work, the clients enjoyed me."

"(Later) I went to work as a Senior social worker...I worked with some pretty damaged youngsters on the street, sort of around Soho, places like that...I was asked to apply as a residential social worker...here I was in an institution again, feeling very comfortable with it, but also feeling in touch with some of the feelings of the kids in there, because I knew what it was like...I set up my own childcare consultancy, which went well.. at a meeting a woman attacked me (in a very nice way!) for not doing more about my disability, was I denying my disability? - and so on....so I did some work and research and I developed a course about Disability and the Law...so from that time, to date, I've been running my consultancy about disability issues."

By the beginning of their professional careers, both Sarah Scott and Ray Harrison-Graham had 'come out' as deaf people. This new identity led them both to the point where they would meet. This is how Sarah describes it:

"It wasn't difficult for me at all, when I joined this deaf company. It made sense to me immediately. There were deaf and hearing people there. I had to learn the language, but it didn't take long. To everyone else it may have seemed long, but not to me....towards the end of my time there I knew about the play 'Children of a Lesser God' (COALG). And I knew that was the next step for me....I was offered a place as understudy in 'Children of a Lesser God'. It was a natural progression for me and I was with the show for three years. This was good experience."

"I went for a month to my first job in Birmingham. It was a 'theatre in education' (TiE) type of job....the point when I came in contact with deaf culture, in any big sense, was through 'Children of a Lesser God'. I had an awareness that it was there, it was a real turning point...I was working with a company doing Macbeth. They were casting 'COALG'...they were asking

Sarah Scott

if I knew of any deaf actors, because I'd lied to them as well about my deafness. I eventually had to tell them I was 'hard of hearing', because in the play I had a lot of entrances where I couldn't see the people on the stage, so they were cueing me by tapping me on the shoulder....the character I played happened to be quite political....around this time I saw a video of signed song and I knew it was something for me."

For Diane, pursuance of satisfactory employment led her across the Atlantic and eventually to the discovery of a new culture - disability culture.

"I was sitting with a friend one evening, she turned to me and asked me if I considered myself as disabled. She worked at

> Artsline and she was organising a sort of disability cabaret and she had thought of me, but she wasn't sure. She knew I had Epilepsy and how I related to it. But I didn't think of myself as a disabled person. I mean I could get on the bus and so on... however, I performed this Epilepsy material that had been bubbling around in my subconscious for a long time...I did this performance and it went extremely well. About six months after Sarah Scott at LDAF contacted me for 'Newcomers Night', I revamped my material, made it longer and better....I was kind of a hit...so slowly I was being asked to perform."

Although Michael Turner tried initially to avoid an employment career overtly concerned with disability, he has found his way into a very pivotal post in a highly politicised organisation run by disabled people. That's not to say there weren't a few hiccoughs along the way - mainly to do with working for an organisation which exists for disabled people but is not run by them.

> "I worked as a trainee at the Arts Centre and that gave me a lot of confidence ....having been to University I thought there would be no problem with employment. I had a good degree, why should there be problems? I thought people would judge me on my academic accomplishments and not be prejudiced by my disability.....later my work for one organisation seemed to go well, but it became clear to me that it was very able-bodied based. There were a few other disabled persons, but at a very low level, mostly menial jobs..."

> "I do prefer working for smaller organisations, though I believe about two thirds of disabled people today get a better and more positive work experience in smaller environments. It's much easier to be oneself...it's true most of the people I work with nowadays, on a day-to-day basis, are mostly untrained; but I do expect the quality of the work assigned to them to be given greater levels of respect and dignity."

In contrast, Julie Turner began her career working with disabled people in a setting which many of our community would seek to avoid, namely a day centre.

> "I was prepared to find that getting a job would be difficult, so after the third interview I was surprised to be offered a job with the London Borough of Hammersmith as a Centre Worker in a day centre for disabled people. Many people think working with disabled people is an easy option - no way! It took a long time for clients to see me as a competent member of staff ...and people did not want to work with me. I had one client with a similar degree of Cerebral Palsy to mine who became extremely resentful of my lifestyle. After some time, clients began to see the benefits of working with me ...I feel it is the type of person someone is, rather than whether a person is disabled or not. After two years as a Centre worker I became Assistant Manager."

People with learning difficulties always have the hardest battle of conviction to win. Roger Brooksby might not have found a steady job yet, but he has an occupation - putting forward self-advocacy for people with learning difficulties by speaking at conferences and seminars. Sadly, his experience of the job market has been a reflection of the low-grade tasks commonly given to people of his constituency.

> "I finished a bit of school. When I got older I went to work at Oxfam. I worked on the till and got to serve people. I enjoyed this, meeting people. It was nice to work and get a bit of money in my pocket. I like the work at Oxfam, I like helping people with Charities. I have moved on from that and now I have been helping at another charity shop as a manual relief. I get a little money and go around to different places. I like helping people when I can."

Roger Brooksby

Of all our group, probably the person who has had the widest experience of employment is a self-confessed nomad, he had just settled down after many adventures to a secure occupation as a theatre consultant when M.E. entered his life. Let Paddy's words explain the impact.

> "The thing about contracting M.E. is ...you suddenly lose everything you have taken for granted. I lost a great many of my mental faculties. I had great difficulty speaking, I couldn't read properly...I was pointed in the direction of the Arts Council's Arts and Disability Monitoring Committee...and from then on it was terribly, terribly emotional..it sounds like a

cliche, but the very beginnings of meeting disabled people was a growing sense of family, the growing sense of education and learning."

Libby and I have different impairments but we share the same career - television. While Libby was at University she was visited by a television producer investigating life for disabled people on campus.

"...early on I knew I wanted to be in production not presentation. I did find presenting great fun. I enjoyed it. But it is a bit superficial, a bit boring. I worked with disabled and non-disabled people during that time and that was a good experience. Working with disabled people in a small office was something I had not done before...I worked with someone who was very politically correct. She put me in my place if I got it wrong."

I didn't wait for television to come to me. I went to it. After seeing all those International Year programmes that were not made by disabled people I saw 'We Won't Go Away' - a documentary made by the Link team. It was real 'Road to Damascus' material because the programme was not just about disabled persons but by disabled persons. Here, at last, was something I wanted to and knew I could, do. Following a programme made for the Community Programmes Unit I relentlessly pursued television, and still do.

In common with the rest of the 'Lifetimes' group my employment record is still not complete. A chapter yet to be written.

I began this chapter by stating how prejudices, stereotypes and misconceptions intervene to the detriment of disabled people's employment. Now to tackle another myth. Prepare to be shocked, because disabled people are NOT asexual.

Chapter 8

Experiences: Sexuality

This chapter shouldn't be here. Sexuality should not be an issue. In the disability community itself sexuality is not an issue. Indeed it only becomes contentious when the need arises to convince others.

The need to convince others takes more than one form. For some time I had the illusion that non-disabled people who are gay men or lesbians would take less convincing than disabled people who shared their sexual orientation. Not so, apparently lesbians and gay men have an uphill battle even just to find solidarity let alone to find a partner.

The heterosexual need to convince is no less easily overcome. The 'Lifetimes' group have all experienced the complications associated with other people's attitudes. No-one has been thwarted by these attitudes.

I asked all our 'Lifetimers' whether sexuality was an issue and, if so, for whom? Libby Cross said...

> "Yes. I think sexuality is an issue. There are too many people out there who think disabled people don't have relationships, or shouldn't have relationships - and who are surprised if you are in a relationship. Most people assume, if you are a woman, and you are disabled and in a relationship, that the man is doing you a favour, or he just couldn't get anyone else. Or if you are a man, they get relationships because women feel sorry for them."

> "There was a prime candidate with whom I went to University, he could pull women like nobody I've seen in my life. He had an effective technique which really worked, the 'mother me, I'm disabled' routine. But there is a danger in this sort of manipulation. They seem to exploit the novelty aspect."

That's one thing I've never tried and wouldn't want to. Not just on principle, but because the last thing you want in a relationship is patronisation. However, she went on to give an anecdote to which I can relate.

> "I remember going to a disco once. shortly after I had come home from hospital. This guy came up to me, absolutely mortal, completely out of it - huge beer belly, breath like you wouldn't believe. He leaned over me and said, 'C'mon luv. I'm your best bet tonight'. I just thought 'I can't cope with this'. But we seem to be targets for this type of attitude. The idea of a disabled person as a sexual partner is quite an attractive one to a certain kind of person."

"You're my best bet ?! You've got to be joking. I'd have a better time with King Kong!"

That happens to me too. If I'm in a mixed crowd and anyone is getting particularly alcoholic you can bet your life they make for me - like bees round a honeypot, and occasionally they'll be female!

Now for a man's view. Here's Phil Friend's perspective.

"I had several relationships where sex had been a possibility, but where, in fact, I rejected it. Yes, I rejected it. The reasons I gave women were that I didn't feel it was right before marriage,

> that it wasn't helpful to have children outside of wedlock, that I respected them too much and that we ought to control ourselves."
>
> "All of that was about not showing my legs, it was a complete cop-out. I was absolutely shit scared of letting them see me undressed. So I gave them all this crap about what a wonderfully responsible man I was. I was terrified they wouldn't like the look of me. It was a physical issue. The way I got over it, finally, was to make love to a disabled woman."
>
> "I was offered the opportunity to sleep with a disabled woman, to whom I am eternally grateful. The question I had about my sexual life was different from able-bodied men. It wasn't that I was more, or less, secure - it was, could I physically do it? It became a real source of concern to me. Was I able, with Polio, in the sense that I've got it, to be a competent lover?"
>
> "But then I met this disabled woman. She invited me back to her place, we had a few beers together, then she invited me back to her bed - and it was lovely."

Lest Phil comes over as a typical boorish male let's hear his views on more general aspects of sexuality.

> "Before we discuss sexuality as an issue for disability, we have to look at sexuality as an issue for everyone. Now I happen to be male. In the generation in which I grew up sex and sexuality had a role and a place. There were expectations....I've sat and talked with able-bodied men and they have just as many hang-ups about sex as I did. They may not be perceived in terms of a physicality, as by people with a physical disability - and from this view stems the disabled person's perception of his or her own disability with a regard to how she or he may see themselves."

One of the issues for disabled people associated with sexuality is connected with choice of partners - do we choose a disabled partner on the grounds that they need no convincing and therefore are approachable or do we choose non-disabled partners on the grounds that to do otherwise is the soft option - or do we just go with the flow? When Ailsa Fairly was at the Blind School for Girls she was under no illusion as to how she should choose.

> "There are so many issues, aren't there. Sexuality, I mean. I would sound pretty naive to say it wasn't an issue. There are all sorts of issues around visually impaired women, for example. At an all-girls school there's a sense of, as you go out into the world, you've made it if you marry a sighted man. And if you get involved with a blind man then you've failed."

For most people the impairment itself is an irrelevance compared to diverting the prejudices of others' attitudes. However, for Genie Cosmas, M.S. did play a part.

> "One thing I noticed after getting M.S. was that my sensitivity, sexually, has decreased. It worried me for ages. But once I stopped worrying about it, and just enjoyed it, there are moments of incredible pleasure. I mean you don't have to have an orgasm every time you have sex. It ceased to be a problem, it's only a problem if you take notice of what the newspapers and magazines say should be the case."

Diane, too, has something to say about her impairment and sexuality.

> "But there are some women who are affected. They have been known to have seizures after orgasm. And they have been faced with the decision of not having orgasms. Now this is something I think is very difficult. I would love to have these women interviewed. But the main thing is they don't tell their lovers this. They hide it. Now, that's bad. This woman actually says

Diane Pungartnik

> she lets him do what he has to do, pretends that she has had an orgasm. Then she excuses herself and cools down so that she won't have a seizure. I think that is really terrible, and I'm sure it's not that uncommon. Epilepsy is very idiosyncratic. I'm sure that's a big problem. It's not just how you are viewed as a sexual person. It's the fact that epilepsy is interfering with your sexual life. This hasn't been a problem for me so far."

As for me, personal relationships are the least successful parts of my life. Lack of opportunity breeds lack of experience. And lack of experience breeds lack of confidence. To complete the vicious circle, lack of confidence means you're less likely to find an opportunity and you're more likely to make a mess of it when the opportunity arises. I have no problems knowing my sexual self. The problem lies in convincing others.

Others in the group have fortunately been more successful than me. Genie, Phil and Ailsa are married. Michael and Julie have a child, as have Genie and her husband. Phil is the father of four, so how does being a parent and a disabled person mix? And since parenting is part of the complexity of the family issue, how have the relatives of our 'Lifetimers' reacted over the years?

Chapter 9

Experiences: Family and parenting

This book is about twelve people, including myself. Between us we have twenty-six siblings, fourteen brothers and twelve sisters. That latter statistic does not include myself because I am an only child. My father too had no brothers or sisters. The only contemporaries I have in the family are three cousins. So, how do families react to having a disabled person amongst them? Does the attitude change all the time?

Libby told me.

> "It's interesting to see how my family's reaction to my disability has changed over the years. My mum is much more educated now. When I graduated, she said to someone (and I could have killed her for saying this) 'Hasn't she done well, despite everything?' I thought, I haven't done well despite everything, I've done well! And she couldn't see it. It certainly wasn't despite it. More because of it. I had to prove that I could do better than everyone else, because of it. I had to prove that I

> could do better than everyone else, because they didn't expect me to. But I think my mum now thinks of me much the same way as she did when I was seventeen, before the accident; she thinks of me as just an ordinary person. She despairs of me sometimes. She gets angry at me other times. But at least she does get angry with me now. For such a long time she wouldn't show that she was angry with me. Now she will, and this is really healthy."

> "My brother David and I get on much better. We got on much better after the accident than we did before. He was very upset by the accident, because I was his big sister. I think he was more deeply affected by the accident than he was about our father dying. I was still around and I had changed a lot. But we were both at a difficult age when that happened."

Diane's family had been similarly positive.

> "My family's reaction to me has been good. We make jokes about it, actually. My sister has had diabetes since she was three. So we've had a disabled aspect in the family. There were things she couldn't do. She couldn't eat. She was a bit frailer than I was, emotionally. She was my only sister, we shared a room, we were very close. But it meant that when we started to have an argument, if she started to get excited, I had to be the one to calm down, because she would go off and have an insulin injection. Her diabetes was very uncontrolled. So I grew up in that milieu.... So once I got Epilepsy, it was like I had mine and she had hers. So we joke about it all the time."

But it's not like that for everyone. Here's how Paddy described his family's reaction to his M.E.

> "The response from my family has been difficult. I think most of them haven't come to terms with it because they haven't confronted it. When I first fell ill I was looked after with

Paddy Masefield

enormous patience and very real kindness by a sister-in-law, who had been a nurse. We got into talking a great deal, which I had never done before with any members of my family. I can remember thinking that my family doesn't come to see me very much and that they didn't seem to be working at the problem. But in the family environment in which I grew up there were a number of unwritten taboos. For instance, you never discussed death, certainly never discussed sex and you never discussed politics. Therefore there was absolutely no experience of engaging at first hand with any sort of issue that one might find difficult."

Roger Brooksby told me of how the brother with whom he had gone to school had taken over the reins of authority in the family and that this authority seems to be liberally exercised as far as Roger is concerned.

> "I have a brother and sister. My brother is married and has two children. I have two nieces. My brother will tell me off when he sees me doing something he thinks I shouldn't do, or if he sees me not doing something I should. He tells me often enough that I've got to do it myself, 'cause no one else will do it for you. He tells me for my own good. He pushes me to be more independent. I don't quarrel with him. He tells me I am capable of doing things. I try to do my jobs right. Sometimes he does push me a little hard, and it seems he has a go at me. Sometimes I think he's hard on me, but it goes in one ear and out the other. I don't quarrel. He does frighten me when he speaks with a very loud voice. But he only tells me off for my own good. I mean he's the boss in the house, since my dad's gone."

How did the 'Lifetimes' families react to their offspring getting married and having children themselves? Here's how Ailsa describes her parents' and in-laws' reaction to her marriage with Steve.

> "When I got married, my family's reaction was no problem, really. I remember my grandfather, in my late teens, being very perturbed I might marry a blind man. But I have always been left to do my own thing. My judgment has always been trusted. I was always quite independent; by this point I had my own home. I think my in-laws had never come into contact with disability before. So it took some getting used to at first. Steve made sure they were well informed about me before they met me. I think they are O.K. now, everything is super. It was so important for them not to think I was a helpless sort of person, leaving Steve to do everything. And when they came for their

first weekend visit, I did everything. I cooked, cleaned - everything! Now they must think I'm Superwoman. Things are fine, nothing phases them now. They are very accepting."

Michael Turner's family reacted to his marriage very well.

"My family's reaction to me as a disabled person has always been positive. I'm sure I exceeded their expectations in terms of my independence. With my marriage to Julie, they have been very proud and supportive."

Of our group, five are parents. Perhaps, not surprisingly, all our 'Lifetimers' are more positive about having disabled children than the rest of the population. Here are a few quotes.

Michael and Julie Turner

"Now I am a parent. My parents were very pleased with the birth of the baby. This was certainly beyond their expectations. I'm sure they thought I would not become a dad. Disabled people as parents always seems a big issue. Our daughter is not disabled, but I know I would be a good parent if she was disabled. I mean, being disabled ourselves, we've been there. We know what to expect, we've been through it. But having said that, I don't think I would want a disabled child because I have been through it, and I do know the difficulties disabled people have in society - with the different types of attitude we are faced with from the non-disabled community. But if it happened that I should have a disabled child, I would still be the best parent I could." (Michael)

Genie Cosmas

"When I became pregnant with my M.S., the hospitals did mention that I would have to take extra care....I decided I wanted my birth to be as natural as possible...and it was lovely, in fact...I've actually met people who have had intervention and it has affected their baby. The parents have then had to come to terms with having a disabled child - in turn the children have had to come to terms with disability. Hopefully, when they are grown up and attitudes have changed, their lives will be better...If I had to come to terms with having a disabled child of my own I think I could cope with the problems much better, now I have experienced my own disability." (Genie)

"If I, as a disabled person, had a disabled child I think I could handle it. I mean I can only look at it in terms of my own blindness. For a child to be born to a parent who is also blind is a positive thing for the child. To know I was going to have a child which has a strong possibility to be born blind is not a reason not to have the child." (Ailsa)

"Maybe later on I'll think about being a father, if I get my mum's permission. But that's later on in the future. You never know what life might bring to me. People may wonder if I can look after kids. But I am a person to put me (sic) foot down!." (Roger)

"I am not intending to have children of my own. They say that Epilepsy is not hereditary, but if both parents have it the child is more likely to have it - I quote that in my cabaret because it is so bloody stupid. But that's what it says in the books. I have often thought that if I knew I could give a child of mine Epilepsy, I wouldn't have one. I didn't have it as a child. But I think it must be difficult, I mean I had so much hell for being different, as it was. Because I was allowed to develop freely, I'm much more confident than most women are." (Diane)

"None of our children are disabled. But when Jack was conceived the chances were fairly high that he would be born disabled. Sue was in her forties at the time. We talked a great deal about whether she would consider a termination. If she didn't and the child was impaired, what would we do, and so on? But we decided if the child was born with an impairment it would be tough but we would handle it."

Phil Friend

"I think my kids have got a clear view of the injustices in society, especially concerning disability. In their own way I think they will become people who will do something about it. My kids have already taken a wheelchair into the school assembly to make others aware of the types of oppression disabled people face in everyday society. George, my son, has even sat in my wheelchair, in front of a thousand kids and said,

'I'd like to come to school (in this wheelchair) today but this school isn't accessible'. It was all his own idea. I was terribly proud of him." (Phil)

The first quotation in this chapter was from Roger Brooksby. Roger isn't married but does have a girl-friend and would like to have children. He is very definite on the subject. Maybe if the views of our 'Lifetimers' were spelt out to society generally, perhaps a more positive attitude to people, such as Roger, would evolve.

Not being a parent and having no brothers or sisters has meant my personal input to this chapter has been limited. However, my family's attitude has always been supportive. There's no doubt about it, I only have one person to thank for empowering me to the point where I am now. Here it is in print Mum - thanks for everything!

Chapter 10

Difference of Opinion

Now this book attempts to defy a golden rule of the disability movement. This principle arose in reaction to the traditions of the popular media. There, the tendency had always been to fasten onto a stereotyped image of either stoic heroicism or helpless objects of pity. The only prevailing point of view of the disabled has been: don't look at individuals, look at the community.

'Lifetimes' does both of these things. The people within these pages are individuals in their own right. But are all representative of the community as a whole? It seems to me it is not necessary to deny individuality in order to highlight our common ground.

Given then, that all the people in this book are individual, how do they differ from each other? Firstly, I suppose, reluctantly, it has to be admitted that the difference between us comes from a wide variety of impairments and, of course, reaction to different physical or mental conditions will change.

Another difference comes from the fact that we all originate from different backgrounds (or cultures in Genie's case). Other differences are chosen fields of work. We've all come to the points we're at now by different routes, educationally and socially; though now, our similarities are greater than our differences. Now comes the point of diversion, where we all started from - and how we got there. We have all taken very different paths. So, on a one-to-one basis, we are the results of different influences and forms of conditioning. All the more surprising then, there are similarities to be found.

On reflection, maybe it isn't all that surprising. Disability influences aren't culture specific, nor are they locked on to different impairments. Globally, we have a disabling society and that's why the 'Lifetimers' represent a community as a whole in their responses.

Chapter 11

A Shared Perspective

Whether we are from America, Asia, Scotland, the North of England or the South-East; whether we are involved in the Arts or Television, Equality Training or Public Relations - we all share a great deal.

Firstly, we all constantly belie social expectations of us as deaf or disabled people. Of course, we all have our personal ambitions, it would be foolish to deny it. But it's not the selfish need for success that drives us, in the main. While, undoubtedly, most of us are trying to carve our own niches, we were also motivated by the need to make a point or two on behalf of our community as a whole, in the face of our disabling society.

Moreover, we don't do it at the cost of our identity. Roger speaks at conferences and seminars as a testimony to how people with learning difficulties don't need others to speak on their behalf. Phil Friend is an Equality Trainer aiming to reduce the disabling attitudes of those who he trains. Libby Cross and I work in disability television and our work is informed by the fact that we are disabled people. Similarly, the art works of Ray, Sarah, Genie and Diane are also informed by their positive sense of self-identity. Paddy is heavily involved in disability arts administration and chooses to be so because he has entirely accommodated his new identity. Julie and Michael Turner work with disabled people in ways which are mutually supportive.

It's not that we're content with the way we are, still less is it a matter of coping. We are all proud of our identity; individually we aim to assist the progress of disabled people in the community. We can do that by example, none of us particularly want to be role models, although we could all be so. We could assist this progress by combining our talents - one way this is already done is through Disability Arts, often given coverage in television programming. We are all part of a movement for change.

But will change happen? What are the prospects, not only for individuals, but, more importantly, for our community? Dare we look with optimism beyond our 'Lifetimes'?

Chapter 12

Conclusions

I asked all our 'Lifetimers' for their hopes and opinions on the future. Here's what they said.

> "I would like to see deaf and disabled people and their art integrated into the mainstream. I would also like to see access, not just physical but in education and jobs, as 'part of the norm'." (Genie)

> "I would like to see things change for people like me in the future. I would like people with learning difficulties to get the opportunity to go out to work for themselves, working at different places. I think the government should try to change the laws so that people with learning difficulties can have a chance." (Roger)

Roger Brooksby

"That we cease to be freaks and objects of curiosity to 'normal' society; are recognised as individuals not as a clump of 'the disabled'; that we cease to be the recipients of charity and start being the active enjoyers of rights....the disabled people in Germany are terribly fearful it is all going to happen again. They feel the dignity of their lives has not been recognised and will not be recognised. And it won't change. If you were to ask me before (my trip to Berlin) I would have been optimistic....the image of disability is so deeply rooted as a negative one here in Britain, with so many disabled people. Unless they develop some sort of political awareness, they will continue to see their lives as negative. The disability movement has got to admit there is an individual, personal experience to disability... We have to get this debate going, we really do." (Libby)

"I would hope, in the next five years, as disabled people, we get anti-discrimination legislation and protection in the areas of employment, access, education and training etc. This is something I want for myself and other disabled people. I'm not prepared to wait another twenty-odd years for it - i.e. be patient." (Ailsa)

"I would like to see anti-discrimination legislation, integrated education, accessible transport, jobs, leisure and a single disability benefit." (Phil)

Phil Friend

"I would like to see Deaf drama schools. To see deaf actors working professionally and on an equal basis to hearing people. To help make Deaf theatre a respected art in its own right. One of the main problems with our society is when it comes to disability, so many people don't realise they are doing wrong. Unlike racism. Until people realise that disabled people's problems and desires are not solved by putting 10p in a plastic box, we will continue to suffer oppression." (Ray)

"My desire would be to have legislation for disability rights and medical recognition of M.E. The creation of original, inspiring and communicative art work and art forms (especially for people with learning difficulties) which will arise from disability arts; which would change the perceptions of the whole arts world. Finally, proper benefit levels to offer dignity in place of begging." (Paddy)

"We have to live in hope that change can be made real, and for the right reasons." (Sarah)

"To rid society of its terrible and deep fear of non-conformity; when 'normality' ceases to be worshipped, disabled people will be a lot better off." (Diane)

"Total integration." (Julie)

"Greater integration of disabled people and more awareness among disabled people ourselves of what we've got in common and what we can achieve....I think having come this far, having dealt with so many disabled people and with so many attitudes towards disabled people I can never go backwards. From this point I can only go forwards. I would certainly not go back without a fight." (Michael)

There's not much else I can add to that. Although to everyone in this book some degree of positive change has happened during our 'Lifetimes', not one of them is contented. Our society still has much to learn and to do. As Libby points out, there is reason to suspect that in some parts of the world even fascism hasn't been completely licked yet. But, even with this note of pessimism, none of us are willing to relent.

There are over six million disabled people in Britain. I have no doubt that some people will say that the twelve people in this book are not typical of most of the disabled population. In one respect maybe that's true; simply because we are all proactive and able to articulate what's wrong with our society and are able to do something about it. But if we, in this book, are not entirely representative of the majority of our community, that is not to say that we are oblivious to the day-to-day existence of that majority. After all, if most people lack the aspirations shared by those in this book, this is, in itself, the most damning consequence of our disabling society. And that's what we're all fighting against. We defy second-class expectations, we work for our community and with our community - and that's how it will probably continue.

Nothing about the future can be certain. But of one thing, at least, I am sure. Remembering the title of the television programme that changed my life, and speaking on behalf of disabled people everywhere, during and beyond our 'Lifetimes' - we won't go away.